Sunday Prayer for Catechists

2025–2026

Daniel J. Allen

LTP

Nihil Obstat
Deacon David Keene, PHD
Chancellor
Archdiocese of Chicago
December 5, 2024

Imprimatur
Most Rev. Robert G. Casey
Vicar General
Archdiocese of Chicago
December 5, 2024

Sunday Prayer for Catechists is based in part on the pattern established in *Children's Daily Prayer* by Elizabeth McMahon Jeep.

This book was edited by Rachel Espinoza. Michael A. Dodd was the production editor, and Juan Alberto Castillo was the cover designer and production artist.

Cover art by Anna Manhart. Interior art by Kari Nicholls.

Printed in the United States of America

ISBN: 978-1-61671-819-0

SPC26

Lord God,
source of all wisdom and knowledge,
you sent your Son, Jesus Christ,
to live among us
and to proclaim his message of faith, hope,
and love to all nations.
In your goodness,
strengthen all catechists with your gifts,
that they may teach the Church by word
and example
the truth that comes from you.
We ask this through Christ our Lord. Amen.

(*Prayer adapted from the Book of Blessings.*)

May the Lord be with you as you work with the young people you are called to serve. We thank you for your ministry.

TABLE OF CONTENTS

September 7, 2025
TWENTY-THIRD SUNDAY IN ORDINARY TIME

✚ *In the name of the Father, and of the Son, and of the Holy Spirit.*

Gospel
Luke 14:25, 27–33

Great crowds were traveling with Jesus, and he turned and addressed them. "Whoever does not carry his own cross and come after me cannot be my disciple. Which of you wishing to construct a tower does not first sit down and calculate the cost to see if there is enough for its completion? Otherwise, after laying the foundation and finding himself unable to finish the work the onlookers should laugh at him and say, 'This one began to build but did not have the resources to finish.' Or what king marching into battle would not first sit down and decide whether with ten thousand troops he can successfully oppose another king advancing upon him with twenty thousand troops? But if not, while he is still far away, he will send a delegation to ask for peace terms. In the same way, anyone of you who does not renounce all his possessions cannot be my disciple."

Reflection
As a new catechetical year begins, I find myself thinking about Jesus' examples and adding one of my own: "What catechist enters the classroom without a lesson plan and expects a message to get through?" Indeed, following Jesus and serving in catechetical ministry requires careful planning and true dedication, and our students can tell when our hearts are not fully committed. We pray that all those who pass along the faith will be filled with patience, steadfastness, and zeal this year, modeling to all students and parents a deep and abiding love for the Lord in all things.

✚ *In the name of the Father, and of the Son, and of the Holy Spirit.*

SEPTEMBER 14, 2025
FEAST OF THE EXALTATION OF THE HOLY CROSS

✚ *In the name of the Father, and of the Son, and of the Holy Spirit.*

GOSPEL

John 3:13–17

Jesus said to Nicodemus: "No one has gone up to heaven except the one who has come down from heaven, the Son of Man. And just as Moses lifted up the serpent in the desert, so must the Son of Man be lifted up, so that everyone who believes in him may have eternal life."

For God so loved the world that he gave his only Son, so that everyone who believes in him might not perish but might have eternal life. For God did not send his Son into the world to condemn the world, but that the world might be saved through him.

REFLECTION

As a child, I remember seeing "John 3:16" written on homemade posters held up by fans during televised sporting events. What is it about this verse that makes it so captivating and so memorable? I think the verse has become so well known and popular because it is essentially a summary of Jesus' mission on Earth. If someone were completely new to Christianity—and seeking understanding like Nicodemus—this verse would be a very good starting point! This week, help your students to reflect on this verse, for it conveys the heart of the Gospel message ("God so loved . . . ") and the call to believe in Jesus, who gave his life so that we might have eternal life.

✚ *In the name of the Father, and of the Son, and of the Holy Spirit.*

SEPTEMBER 21, 2025
TWENTY-FIFTH SUNDAY IN ORDINARY TIME

✚ *In the name of the Father, and of the Son, and of the Holy Spirit.*

GOSPEL

Luke 16:10–13

Jesus said to his disciples, "The person who is trustworthy in very small matters is also trustworthy in great ones; and the person who is dishonest in very small matters is also dishonest in great ones. If, therefore, you are not trustworthy with dishonest wealth, who will trust you with true wealth? If you are not trustworthy with what belongs to another, who will give you what is yours? No servant can serve two masters. He will either hate one and love the other, or be devoted to one and despise the other. You cannot serve both God and mammon."

REFLECTION

We are all stewards of both insignificant and significant things. The insignificant things include our money and our possessions. The significant things last beyond death: our loved ones and our souls. How much time, energy, and focus do we give to insignificant things? If we are not careful, these things can take up all of our attention. Conversely, how much do we focus on the truly important things in life—the people God has given us? Those with whom we interact on a daily basis, including our families, friends, and students, are all beloved children of God. When we start to view people and things from God's perspective, we realize how much we have been given and how our priorities must be ordered.

✚ *In the name of the Father, and of the Son, and of the Holy Spirit.*

SEPTEMBER 28, 2025
TWENTY-SIXTH SUNDAY IN ORDINARY TIME

✚ *In the name of the Father, and of the Son, and of the Holy Spirit.*

GOSPEL

Luke 16:19–25

Jesus said to the Pharisees: "There was a rich man who dressed in purple garments and fine linen and dined sumptuously each day. And lying at his door was a poor man named Lazarus, covered with sores, who would gladly have eaten his fill of the scraps that fell from the rich man's table. Dogs even used to come and lick his sores. When the poor man died, he was carried away by angels to the bosom of Abraham. The rich man also died and was buried, and from the netherworld, where he was in torment, he raised his eyes and saw Abraham far off and Lazarus at his side. And he cried out, 'Father Abraham, have pity on me. Send Lazarus to dip the tip of his finger in water and cool my tongue, for I am suffering torment in these flames.' Abraham replied, 'My child, remember that you received what was good during your lifetime while Lazarus likewise received what was bad; but now he is comforted here, whereas you are tormented.'"

REFLECTION

While we live in a time of general material wealth, there are still many around us who are in need. Our Gospel reading calls us to respond differently than the rich man did and to see Jesus' face in those forgotten and overlooked by society. Of course, the poverty we see today goes beyond the material realm. Too many in our world are lacking in spiritual riches, having never been given the gifts of our faith. As catechists, we are called to minister to those who are in need in this way. Ask God for the grace to be more aware of the needs around us so that no one is left unnoticed and unloved by others.

✚ *In the name of the Father, and of the Son, and of the Holy Spirit.*

October 5, 2025
TWENTY-SEVENTH SUNDAY IN ORDINARY TIME

✚ *In the name of the Father, and of the Son, and of the Holy Spirit.*

Gospel

Luke 17:5–6

The apostles said to the Lord, "Increase our faith." The Lord replied, "If you have faith the size of a mustard seed, you would say to this mulberry tree, 'Be uprooted and planted in the sea,' and it would obey you."

Reflection

Like the apostles in today's reading, we might find ourselves desiring an increase in faith. The endless news cycle is filled with so many of humanity's shortcomings that it can leave us discouraged about our human potential or doubtful of God's love. We yearn to see small acts of faith—even those the size of a mustard seed—that will bolster our spirits. But when we pay close attention, we do see such powerful things. I think back to the times in the classroom when a child who seemed otherwise disinterested latched on to a tenet of faith and engaged with the material and peers in a new way. Indeed, there are many small moments that help us to realize God's presence and that can give us restored hope as we work to be humble conduits of God's love to others.

✚ *In the name of the Father, and of the Son, and of the Holy Spirit.*

October 12, 2025
TWENTY-EIGHTH SUNDAY IN ORDINARY TIME

✚ *In the name of the Father, and of the Son, and of the Holy Spirit.*

Gospel

Luke 17:11–19

As Jesus continued his journey to Jerusalem, he traveled through Samaria and Galilee. As he was entering a village, ten lepers met him. They stood at a distance from him and raised their voices, saying, "Jesus, Master! Have pity on us!" And when he saw them, he said, "Go show yourselves to the priests." As they were going they were cleansed. And one of them, realizing he had been healed, returned, glorifying God in a loud voice; and he fell at the feet of Jesus and thanked him. He was a Samaritan. Jesus said in reply, "Ten were cleansed, were they not? Where are the other nine? Has none but this foreigner returned to give thanks to God?" Then he said to him, "Stand up and go; your faith has saved you."

Reflection

As catechists, we can sometimes be discouraged by the seeming lack of effectiveness of our ministry. At times, we may wonder whether we are wasting our time trying to pass along the faith. And yet, in today's Gospel, even the Son of God only seems to have a ten percent success rate! This passage, though, is not really about rates of conversion or any other metric; it is about the healing love of God and the human response. At different moments of our lives, we have been the nine who lacked gratitude and the one who returned to give thanks. It is up to us to be mindful of how much God has done for us, and to respond in gratitude. It is from our own example of grateful living that we may inspire others to do the same.

✚ *In the name of the Father, and of the Son, and of the Holy Spirit.*

October 19, 2025
TWENTY-NINTH SUNDAY IN ORDINARY TIME

✚ *In the name of the Father, and of the Son, and of the Holy Spirit.*

Gospel

Luke 18:1–8

Jesus told his disciples a parable about the necessity for them to pray always without becoming weary. He said, "There was a judge in a certain town who neither feared God nor respected any human being. And a widow in that town used to come to him and say, 'Render a just decision for me against my adversary.' For a long time the judge was unwilling, but eventually he thought, 'While it is true that I neither fear God nor respect any human being, because this widow keeps bothering me I shall deliver a just decision for her lest she finally come and strike me.'" The Lord said, "Pay attention to what the dishonest judge says. Will not God then secure the rights of his chosen ones who call out to him day and night? Will he be slow to answer them? I tell you, he will see to it that justice is done for them speedily. But when the Son of Man comes, will he find faith on earth?"

Reflection

In our human experience, there are moments (usually, enjoyable ones) that seem to speed along so fast that we are surprised at how quickly the time has passed. Then there are the moments (usually, the challenging ones) that seem to drag on forever. At times it can feel like time is standing still as we wait for God to answer our most earnest prayers. When our loved ones are suffering or our students are struggling in some way, it can seem like God is not hearing us. In those moments, let us take our inspiration from the widow in today's story. Her persistence was finally rewarded, and we know that we have a more compassionate judge than the one who answered her.

✚ *In the name of the Father, and of the Son, and of the Holy Spirit.*

October 26, 2025
THIRTIETH SUNDAY IN ORDINARY TIME

✚ *In the name of the Father, and of the Son, and of the Holy Spirit.*

Gospel
Luke 18:9–14

Jesus addressed this parable to those who were convinced of their own righteousness and despised everyone else. "Two people went up to the temple area to pray; one was a Pharisee and the other was a tax collector. The Pharisee took up his position and spoke this prayer to himself, 'O God, I thank you that I am not like the rest of humanity—greedy, dishonest, adulterous—or even like this tax collector. I fast twice a week, and I pay tithes on my whole income.' But the tax collector stood off at a distance and would not even raise his eyes to heaven but beat his breast and prayed, 'O God, be merciful to me a sinner.' I tell you, the latter went home justified, not the former; for whoever exalts himself will be humbled, and the one who humbles himself will be exalted."

Reflection
There is a constant temptation to compare ourselves with others. We fall into the trap of wondering about other people's financial situations, the happiness of their relationships, their health and physical fitness, and perhaps, as catechists, their effectiveness in the classroom. What does all of this comparison gain for us? If we listen to today's Gospel, we realize that we gain nothing of value. Instead, it is a much better use of our time and energy to examine our relationship with God, to accept his mercy, and to recommit ourselves to the ministry God has given us. God will then look upon us with compassion and love.

✚ *In the name of the Father, and of the Son, and of the Holy Spirit.*

NOVEMBER 2, 2025
COMMEMORATION OF ALL THE FAITHFUL DEPARTED

✚ *In the name of the Father, and of the Son, and of the Holy Spirit.*

GOSPEL
John 14:1–6

Jesus said to his disciples: “Do not let your hearts be troubled. You have faith in God; have faith also in me. In my Father’s house there are many dwelling places. If there were not, would I have told you that I am going to prepare a place for you? And if I go and prepare a place for you, I will come back again and take you to myself, so that where I am you also may be. Where I am going you know the way.” Thomas said to him, “Master, we do not know where you are going; how can we know the way?” Jesus said to him, “I am the way and the truth and the life. No one comes to the Father except through me.”

Note: This is one possible option of the Gospel reading for today.

REFLECTION
My first experience of death was as a young child after my grandfather’s wake. After all of the guests had gone, and only the extended family remained, I found myself alone with my grandfather’s body. I remember praying and asking for him to wake up, wishing that this painful experience would end. When that did not happen, I had to look for the consolation offered by our faith that our story does not end in death. It is this trust in God’s salvation that has sustained me during other moments of grief and loss. When our religious education students encounter some of life’s hard lessons, may we be a voice of understanding and compassion that shows them the way to Jesus, the one who offers them lasting hope.

✚ *In the name of the Father, and of the Son, and of the Holy Spirit.*

NOVEMBER 9, 2025
FEAST OF THE DEDICATION OF THE LATERAN BASILICA

✚ *In the name of the Father, and of the Son, and of the Holy Spirit.*

GOSPEL *John 2:13–17*

Since the Passover of the Jews was near, Jesus went up to Jerusalem. He found in the temple area those who sold oxen, sheep, and doves, as well as the money-changers seated there. He made a whip out of cords and drove them all out of the temple area, with the sheep and the oxen, and spilled the coins of the money-changers and overturned their tables, and to those who sold doves he said, "Take these out of here, and stop making my Father's house a marketplace." His disciples recalled the words of Scripture, *Zeal for your house will consume me.*

REFLECTION

Being part of the building of a church is a unique experience. In addition to financial concerns, members of the building committee often hold long discussions about art, design, catechetical elements, and the placement of key objects. Eventually these discussions fade, and what is left is the physical building that houses the community's worship and that serves as a silent teacher of the faithful long after the builders are gone. Traveling to churches that were built centuries ago—like the Lateran Basilica we celebrate today—provides an opportunity to share the same faith that prompted other believers to build such tremendous edifices designed to lift hearts and minds to God.

✚ *In the name of the Father, and of the Son, and of the Holy Spirit.*

November 16, 2025
THIRTY-THIRD SUNDAY IN ORDINARY TIME

✚ *In the name of the Father, and of the Son, and of the Holy Spirit.*

Gospel

Luke 21:5–9

While some people were speaking about how the temple was adorned with costly stones and votive offerings, Jesus said, "All that you see here—the days will come when there will not be left a stone upon another stone that will not be thrown down."

Then they asked him, "Teacher, when will this happen? And what sign will there be when all these things are about to happen?" He answered, "See that you not be deceived, for many will come in my name, saying, 'I am he,' and 'The time has come.' Do not follow them! When you hear of wars and insurrections, do not be terrified; for such things must happen first, but it will not immediately be the end."

Reflection

As we near the end of the liturgical year, we encounter readings that sound ominous and downright fearful. We ourselves live in days that are filled with division and unrest. Where do we find the capacity to put our trust in God and not allow ourselves to be overcome with fear? I find it helpful to look back in history and consider other times when our ancestors in faith experienced great calamity. What must it have been like to see Jesus crucified, loved ones martyred, or the beloved Church in schism? We do not have to look very far to realize that our experiences have connections to the past, and we can find hope and inspiration in the ones who persevered beyond the challenges they faced. As we guide our students, we are called to bear witness to all that the Church has already overcome.

✚ *In the name of the Father, and of the Son, and of the Holy Spirit.*

November 23, 2025
SOLEMNITY OF OUR LORD JESUS CHRIST, KING OF THE UNIVERSE

✚ *In the name of the Father, and of the Son, and of the Holy Spirit.*

Gospel

Luke 23:35–43

The rulers sneered at Jesus and said, "He saved others, let him save himself if he is the chosen one, the Christ of God." Even the soldiers jeered at him. As they approached to offer him wine they called out, "If you are King of the Jews, save yourself." Above him there was an inscription that read, "This is the King of the Jews."

Now one of the criminals hanging there reviled Jesus, saying, "Are you not the Christ? Save yourself and us." The other, however, rebuking him, said in reply, "Have you no fear of God, for you are subject to the same condemnation? And indeed, we have been condemned justly, for the sentence we received corresponds to our crimes, but this man has done nothing criminal." Then he said, "Jesus, remember me when you come into your kingdom." He replied to him, "Amen, I say to you, today you will be with me in Paradise."

Reflection

When the Jewish people considered who the Messiah might be, many imagined a powerful political or military leader. Instead, Jesus came as a helpless infant to a poor family. When thinking about who would make a great king, we ourselves aren't likely to consider a man executed on a cross. But as we know, this is exactly who our king is, and his dominion is stronger than death. Our calling as religious educators is to introduce this king to each person entrusted to our care. As we come before him in worship, let us trust that God's plan and reign are far superior to anything we can think or imagine.

✚ *In the name of the Father, and of the Son, and of the Holy Spirit.*

November 30, 2025
FIRST SUNDAY OF ADVENT

✚ *In the name of the Father, and of the Son, and of the Holy Spirit.*

Gospel

Matthew 24:37–44

Jesus said to his disciples, "As it was in the days of Noah, so it will be at the coming of the Son of Man. In those days before the flood, they were eating and drinking, marrying and giving in marriage, up to the day that Noah entered the ark. They did not know until the flood came and carried them all away. So will it be also at the coming of the Son of Man. Two men will be out in the field; one will be taken, and one will be left. Two women will be grinding at the mill; one will be taken, and one will be left. Therefore, stay awake! For you do not know on which day your Lord will come. Be sure of this: if the master of the house had known the hour of night when the thief was coming, he would have stayed awake and not let his house be broken into. So too, you also must be prepared, for at an hour you do not expect, the Son of Man will come."

Reflection

The periods of quiet stability in our lives have a way of fooling us into thinking that things will always remain the same. But over time, all of us will face times of transition and painful, unexpected moments that are part of the human experience. Jesus calls us to be prepared for these moments by rooting ourselves in him as our unshakable foundation. If we remain firm in faith, we will not be caught off guard by the trials that may come our way.

✚ *In the name of the Father, and of the Son, and of the Holy Spirit.*

December 7, 2025
SECOND SUNDAY OF ADVENT

✚ *In the name of the Father, and of the Son, and of the Holy Spirit.*

Gospel

Matthew 3:1–6

John the Baptist appeared, preaching in the desert of Judea and saying, "Repent, for the kingdom of heaven is at hand!" It was of him that the prophet Isaiah had spoken when he said: / *A voice of one crying out in the desert, / Prepare the way of the Lord, make straight his paths.* / John wore clothing made of camel's hair and had a leather belt around his waist. His food was locusts and wild honey. At that time Jerusalem, all Judea, and the whole region around the Jordan were going out to him and were being baptized by him in the Jordan River as they acknowledged their sins.

Reflection

I once had the great blessing of traveling to the Holy Land and visiting the Jordan River. Closing my eyes there, I could imagine the scene from today's Gospel playing out in real life. I imagined John the Baptist's unkempt appearance and fiery words resounding in the valley, drawing gasps from the approaching crowds. We might say his teaching methods were unconventional! He was desperately trying to prepare the people for the arrival of the Messiah, and we do something similar during this season of Advent. In our hearts, homes, and classrooms, things change in anticipation of who will soon arrive, but if we only prepare with decorations, we miss the true meaning of this season. We are called to repent, to recommit ourselves to our baptismal promises, and to lead others in waiting for the coming of the Savior, both at Christmas and at the end of time.

✚ *In the name of the Father, and of the Son, and of the Holy Spirit.*

December 8, 2025
THE IMMACULATE CONCEPTION OF THE BLESSED VIRGIN MARY

✚ *In the name of the Father, and of the Son, and of the Holy Spirit.*

Gospel

Luke 1:26–31, 34–38

The angel Gabriel was sent from God to a town of Galilee called Nazareth, to a virgin betrothed to a man named Joseph, of the house of David, and the virgin's name was Mary. And coming to her, he said, "Hail, full of grace! The Lord is with you." But she was greatly troubled at what was said and pondered what sort of greeting this might be. Then the angel said to her, "Do not be afraid, Mary, for you have found favor with God. Behold, you will conceive in your womb and bear a son, and you shall name him Jesus." But Mary said to the angel, "How can this be, since I have no relations with a man?" And the angel said to her in reply, "The Holy Spirit will come upon you, and the power of the Most High will overshadow you. Therefore the child to be born will be called holy, the Son of God. And behold, Elizabeth, your relative, has also conceived a son in her old age, and this is the sixth month for her who was called barren; for nothing will be impossible for God." Mary said, "Behold, I am the handmaid of the Lord. May it be done to me according to your word." Then the angel departed from her.

Reflection

Today we celebrate Mary's immaculate conception, the grace that she was given before birth to be free of original sin. Although she was given this grace as a special gift of God to prepare her for the critical role she would play in our salvation, we also marvel at her willingness to follow God's will, even when the road was uncertain. May her example teach us how to give a fuller yes to all that God may ask of us.

✚ *In the name of the Father, and of the Son, and of the Holy Spirit.*

December 14, 2025
THIRD SUNDAY OF ADVENT

✚ *In the name of the Father, and of the Son, and of the Holy Spirit.*

Gospel

Matthew 11:7–11

As they were going off, Jesus began to speak to the crowds about John, "What did you go out to the desert to see? A reed swayed by the wind? Then what did you go out to see? Someone dressed in fine clothing? Those who wear fine clothing are in royal palaces. Then why did you go out? To see a prophet? Yes, I tell you, and more than a prophet. This is the one about whom it is written: *Behold, I am sending my messenger ahead of you; / he will prepare your way before you.* Amen, I say to you, among those born of women there has been none greater than John the Baptist; yet the least in the kingdom of heaven is greater than he."

Reflection

John the Baptist is one of my favorite saints because he is an inspiration to all those who try to share the message of Christ. Just when John is at the height of human influence, he turns and points to Jesus as the one to follow. John's humility is a great reminder that fame, recognition, and prominence are all fleeting, even in the ministry of evangelization. While we are called to lead people to Jesus with zeal, we eventually take a step back so that people can put even more of their trust in the Lord who loves them perfectly.

✚ *In the name of the Father, and of the Son, and of the Holy Spirit.*

DECEMBER 21, 2025
FOURTH SUNDAY OF ADVENT

✚ *In the name of the Father, and of the Son, and of the Holy Spirit.*

GOSPEL

Matthew 1:18–24

This is how the birth of Jesus Christ came about. When his mother Mary was betrothed to Joseph, but before they lived together, she was found with child through the Holy Spirit. Joseph her husband, since he was a righteous man, yet unwilling to expose her to shame, decided to divorce her quietly. Such was his intention when, behold, the angel of the Lord appeared to him in a dream and said, "Joseph, son of David, do not be afraid to take Mary your wife into your home. For it is through the Holy Spirit that this child has been conceived in her. She will bear a son and you are to name him Jesus, because he will save his people from their sins." All this took place to fulfill what the Lord had said through the prophet: *Behold, the virgin shall be with child and bear a son, / and they shall name him Emmanuel, /* which means "God is with us." When Joseph awoke, he did as the angel of the Lord had commanded him and took his wife into his home.

REFLECTION

I always find it curious that Joseph (despite being the foster father of Jesus) actually has no spoken words in the Gospels. Think of the difficulty we would have being effective catechists without using any words! But as we know, Joseph does not have to be a man of words because he is a man of obedience and action. Even though he had misgivings about the situation at hand, he listened to the counsel of the angel in his dream, inspiring us to trust God's plan even when we are uncertain about it.

✚ *In the name of the Father, and of the Son, and of the Holy Spirit.*

December 25, 2025
SOLEMNITY OF THE NATIVITY OF THE LORD (MASS AT NIGHT)

✚ *In the name of the Father, and of the Son, and of the Holy Spirit.*

Gospel

Luke 2:1–7

In those days a decree went out from Caesar Augustus that the whole world should be enrolled. This was the first enrollment, when Quirinius was governor of Syria. So all went to be enrolled, each to his own town. And Joseph too went up from Galilee from the town of Nazareth to Judea, to the city of David that is called Bethlehem, because he was of the house and family of David, to be enrolled with Mary, his betrothed, who was with child. While they were there, the time came for her to have her child, and she gave birth to her firstborn son. She wrapped him in swaddling clothes and laid him in a manger, because there was no room for them in the inn.

Reflection

What can be said about this sacred night that wiser people have not already said? Nevertheless, we must consider every Christmas of our lives a gift. While the story has not changed, we have changed each time we celebrate this holy moment. Will we allow the Christ child to enter our hearts once again, to allow his holy light to shine through the darkness?

✚ *In the name of the Father, and of the Son, and of the Holy Spirit.*

December 28, 2025
FEAST OF THE HOLY FAMILY OF JESUS, MARY AND JOSEPH

✚ *In the name of the Father, and of the Son, and of the Holy Spirit.*

Gospel

Matthew 2:19–23

When Herod had died, behold, the angel of the Lord appeared in a dream to Joseph in Egypt and said, "Rise, take the child and his mother and go to the land of Israel, for those who sought the child's life are dead." He rose, took the child and his mother, and went to the land of Israel. But when he heard that Archaelaus was ruling over Judea in place of his father Herod, he was afraid to go back there. And because he had been warned in a dream, he departed for the region of Galilee. He went and dwelt in a town called Nazareth, so that what had been spoken through the prophets might be fulfilled, *He shall be called a Nazorean.*

Reflection

The events of Jesus' early childhood were anything but ordinary and peaceful. Following the angel's warning, Joseph took Mary and Jesus to Egypt. Even after Herod's death, fear led the holy family to settle in Galilee rather than Judea. Yet their displacement leads to the fulfilment of another of God's prophecies concerning the Messiah: *He shall be called a Nazorean.* Through these details, we are reminded that even the messiness and hardships that we and our students experience in family life can be used by God to bring about some greater good. Jesus comes with a divine purpose that will be opposed mightily, but nothing can thwart his work of redemption.

✚ *In the name of the Father, and of the Son, and of the Holy Spirit.*

January 1, 2026
SOLEMNITY OF MARY, MOTHER OF GOD

✚ *In the name of the Father, and of the Son, and of the Holy Spirit.*

Gospel
Luke 2:16–21

The shepherds went in haste to Bethlehem and found Mary and Joseph, and the infant lying in the manger. When they saw this, they made known the message that had been told them about this child. All who heard it were amazed by what had been told them by the shepherds. And Mary kept all these things, reflecting on them in her heart. Then the shepherds returned, glorifying and praising God for all they had heard and seen, just as it had been told to them.

When eight days were completed for his circumcision, he was named Jesus, the name given him by the angel before he was conceived in the womb.

Reflection

Today's reading prompts us to consider Mary's immaculate heart and all of the beautiful, painful, and mysterious things she pondered within it. Who could imagine the depth of sadness she carried as her heart was pierced by the sorrowful moments she endured? And what sublime joy she must have felt as she saw and heard of Jesus' great deeds during his public ministry, and especially at his resurrection? As catechists, we invite our students to draw near and to imitate Mary in pondering the life of her Son. May she—whose yes brought Christ into the world—intercede for us as we seek to bring Christ to those we serve!

✚ *In the name of the Father, and of the Son, and of the Holy Spirit.*

January 4, 2026
SOLEMNITY OF THE EPIPHANY OF THE LORD

✚ *In the name of the Father, and of the Son, and of the Holy Spirit.*

Gospel
Matthew 2:1–3, 9–12

When Jesus was born in Bethlehem of Judea, in the days of King Herod, behold, magi from the east arrived in Jerusalem, saying, "Where is the newborn king of the Jews? We saw his star at its rising and have come to do him homage." After their audience with the king they set out. And behold, the star that they had seen at its rising preceded them, until it came and stopped over the place where the child was. They were overjoyed at seeing the star, and on entering the house they saw the child with Mary his mother. They prostrated themselves and did him homage. Then they opened their treasures and offered him gifts of gold, frankincense, and myrrh. And having been warned in a dream not to return to Herod, they departed for their country by another way.

Reflection
Today's Gospel offers a dramatic juxtaposition of characters. First, we consider the humble Magi, who sacrificed greatly to travel to meet and worship Jesus. They honor him with precious gifts and are open to the wisdom of God revealed in a dream. King Herod is a man of crippling insecurity, unable to imagine that another could surpass him in importance. While the wise men are filled with wisdom, Herod is filled with jealous rage that drove him to kill many innocent children. As we consider these two extremes, where do we fall in the continuum between wisdom and foolishness? And as we help our students consider the many voices that clamor for their attention, we pray for the grace to lead them toward righteousness, guiding them to worship the King of Kings.

✚ *In the name of the Father, and of the Son, and of the Holy Spirit.*

JANUARY 11, 2026
FEAST OF THE BAPTISM OF THE LORD

✚ *In the name of the Father, and of the Son, and of the Holy Spirit.*

GOSPEL

Matthew 3:13–17

Jesus came from Galilee to John at the Jordan to be baptized by him. John tried to prevent him, saying, "I need to be baptized by you, and yet, you are coming to me?" Jesus said to him in reply, "Allow it for now, for thus it is fitting for us to fulfill all righteousness." Then he allowed him. After Jesus was baptized, he came up from the water and behold, the heavens were opened for him, and he saw the Spirit of God descending like a dove and coming upon him. And a voice came from the heavens, saying, "This is my beloved Son, with whom I am well pleased."

REFLECTION

Baptisms are beautiful moments for family, friends, and the Christian community to come together to witness someone receiving new life in Christ. When babies are involved, there is a dual excitement about the recent birth and about the baptism. When people are baptized later in life, there is a special kind of inspiration to those who witness it. Any Easter Vigil that includes baptisms is filled with smiles and happy tears, even when we do not know personally those who are baptized. Our rejoicing is due to the fact that another person is following Jesus into the water and into a life of faith, and this is a joy that all who share in catechetical ministry know. Indeed, there is no greater joy than witnessing another seeking to follow Christ!

✚ *In the name of the Father, and of the Son, and of the Holy Spirit.*

January 18, 2026
SECOND SUNDAY IN ORDINARY TIME

✚ *In the name of the Father, and of the Son, and of the Holy Spirit.*

Gospel

John 1:29–34

John the Baptist saw Jesus coming toward him and said, "Behold, the Lamb of God, who takes away the sin of the world. He is the one of whom I said, 'A man is coming after me who ranks ahead of me because he existed before me.' I did not know him, but the reason why I came baptizing with water was that he might be made known to Israel." John testified further, saying, "I saw the Spirit come down like a dove from heaven and remain upon him. I did not know him, but the one who sent me to baptize with water told me, 'On whomever you see the Spirit come down and remain, he is the one who will baptize with the Holy Spirit.' Now I have seen and testified that he is the Son of God."

Reflection

A critical moment of any track relay race is the handing off of the baton. Should a team drop the baton, their chances of winning the race diminish greatly. The final runner, called the anchor, is usually the fastest. Today's reading reminded me of a relay race. John the Baptist has been dutifully carrying out his mission of preparing people for Jesus. When Jesus arrives, John passes the figurative baton, understanding that he has completed his portion of God's salvific work, and it is now Christ the anchor's turn to carry on the mission of our salvation. Unlike a relay race, however, the anchor continues to pass the baton, first to the Holy Spirit and then to the Church. We as catechists are part of this great relay of faith, passing along to the next generation.

✚ *In the name of the Father, and of the Son, and of the Holy Spirit.*

January 25, 2026
THIRD SUNDAY IN ORDINARY TIME

✚ *In the name of the Father, and of the Son, and of the Holy Spirit.*

Gospel

Matthew 4:18–22

As [Jesus] was walking by the Sea of Galilee, he saw two brothers, Simon who is called Peter, and his brother Andrew, casting a net into the sea; they were fishermen. He said to them, "Come after me, and I will make you fishers of men." At once they left their nets and followed him. He walked along from there and saw two other brothers, James, the son of Zebedee, and his brother John. They were in a boat, with their father Zebedee, mending their nets. He called them, and immediately they left their boat and their father and followed him.

Reflection

When we think about the calling of the disciples, it can be easy to miss how significant their leap of faith was. The Gospel tells us that they left their nets and their boats and followed Jesus. Their nets and their boats aren't just physical items: they were the tools that helped them provide food and income for their lives. Yet when Jesus walks along the shore and calls the disciples to a greater task, they leave behind the lesser one. What "nets" might Jesus be calling us to release?

✚ *In the name of the Father, and of the Son, and of the Holy Spirit.*

February 1, 2026
FOURTH SUNDAY IN ORDINARY TIME

✚ *In the name of the Father, and of the Son, and of the Holy Spirit.*

Gospel

Matthew 5:1–12

[Jesus said]: "Blessed are the poor in spirit, / for theirs is the kingdom of heaven. / Blessed are they who mourn, / for they will be comforted. / Blessed are the meek, / for they will inherit the land. / Blessed are they who hunger and thirst for righteousness, / for they will be satisfied. / Blessed are the merciful, / for they will be shown mercy. / Blessed are the clean of heart, / for they will see God. / Blessed are the peacemakers, / for they will be called children of God. / Blessed are they who are persecuted for the sake of righteousness, / for theirs is the kingdom of heaven. / Blessed are you when they insult you and persecute you / and utter every kind of evil against you falsely because of me. / Rejoice and be glad, / for your reward will be great in heaven."

Reflection

The Beatitudes are helpful because they are not simply a list of prohibitions against sinful behavior but positive guidance about how to live. The first several, while not easy, seem like wise and noble ideals that would not take too much convincing to get behind. Toward the end of the list, though, things get quite serious. Being persecuted, insulted, and scorned?! Jesus seems to understand our hesitation and, like a good teacher, knows that we need help to embrace more difficult things. Therefore, he promises great rewards in heaven. Jesus gives us a model for how we might approach sharing difficult truths with our students and reminds us that everything we teach must ultimately point to the great joy that awaits us.

✚ *In the name of the Father, and of the Son, and of the Holy Spirit.*

February 8, 2026
FIFTH SUNDAY IN ORDINARY TIME

✚ *In the name of the Father, and of the Son, and of the Holy Spirit.*

Gospel

Matthew 5:13–16

Jesus said to his disciples: "You are the salt of the earth. But if salt loses its taste, with what can it be seasoned? It is no longer good for anything but to be thrown out and trampled underfoot. You are the light of the world. A city set on a mountain cannot be hidden. Nor do they light a lamp and then put it under a bushel basket; it is set on a lampstand, where it gives light to all in the house. Just so, your light must shine before others, that they may see your good deeds and glorify your heavenly Father."

Reflection

The ability of our human senses to detect very small changes is remarkable: consider the far-off noise heard on a quiet night, the tiniest sliver felt acutely in a finger, or a single whiff of cigarette smoke in a large space. This week's Gospel uses the metaphors of salt and light. Even a small amount of salt can enliven a plain-tasting dish, and a single candle can be seen from a distance in the dark. Our ministry as catechists is not always made up of grandiose gestures. Frequently, it's the small things that we do—our consistency, patience, heartfelt belief, and simple acts of care for our students—that have the greatest effect. By sharing the Good News—in big ways and in small—we bear witness and bring glory to God.

✚ *In the name of the Father, and of the Son, and of the Holy Spirit.*

February 15, 2026

SIXTH SUNDAY IN ORDINARY TIME

✚ *In the name of the Father, and of the Son, and of the Holy Spirit.*

Gospel

Matthew 5:22–22a, 27–28, 33–34a, 37

[Jesus said to his disciples:] "You have heard that it was said to your ancestors, / *You shall not kill; and whoever kills will be liable to judgment.* / But I say to you, whoever is angry with his brother will be liable to judgment.

"You have heard that it was said, / *You shall not commit adultery.* / But I say to you, everyone who looks at a woman with lust has already committed adultery with her in his heart.

"Again, you have heard that it was said to your ancestors, *Do not take a false oath, but make good to the Lord all that you vow.* / But I say to you, do not swear at all. Let your 'Yes' mean 'Yes,' and your 'No' mean 'No.' Anything more is from the evil one."

Reflection

After the snow, ice, and freezing winter, many of our roads are in rough shape by this time of year. Driving around can feel like a strange sort of dodgem game until the road crews can fill the holes or resurface the roads. Though it can seem like potholes appear suddenly, we know that they start out as small cracks. Over time, the combination of water, periodic freezing, and the weight of passing vehicles does the rest. I think that is a good image for us to consider when digesting Jesus' words today and teaching them to others. By rooting out even the smaller instances of sin, we more easily avoid major mistakes and live closer to the freedom God offers us. Thankfully, the mercy of God is available to all who seek it, and any defect, be it great or small, can be restored by God's infinite forgiveness.

✚ *In the name of the Father, and of the Son, and of the Holy Spirit.*

February 22, 2026
FIRST SUNDAY OF LENT

✚ *In the name of the Father, and of the Son, and of the Holy Spirit.*

Gospel

Matthew 4:1–4

Jesus was led by the Spirit into the desert to be tempted by the devil. He fasted for forty days and forty nights, and afterwards he was hungry. The tempter approached and said to him, "If you are the Son of God, command that these stones become loaves of bread." He said in reply, "It is written: *One does not live by bread alone, / but on every word that comes forth from the mouth of God.*"

Reflection

As we follow the fasting and abstinence that the Church asks of us this season, we get a small glimpse into Jesus' sacrifice in the desert. We notice our stomach's grumble, and we resist the urge to consume food freely during these days. If we can get beyond those initial hunger pangs, we may experience a sort of clarity that fasting can create. Instead of thinking about snacking or our next meal, we set those concerns aside for a time and consider matters of a higher order. This is what Jesus accomplishes in the wilderness. He is able to resist the temptations of Satan and instead focus on his Father's will. Are there ways that we or our catechetical students are still tripped up by unholy desires? Do we find ourselves easily distracted by the things of this world and forget to keep our …s on God? We pray that this Lent will be another opportunity …arpen our focus on what truly feeds and sustains us.

… Father, and of the Son, and of the Holy Spirit.

March 1, 2026
SECOND SUNDAY OF LENT

✚ *In the name of the Father, and of the Son, and of the Holy Spirit.*

Gospel

Matthew 17:1–5

Jesus took Peter, James, and John his brother, and led them up a high mountain by themselves. And he was transfigured before them; his face shone like the sun and his clothes became white as light. And behold, Moses and Elijah appeared to them, conversing with him. Then Peter said to Jesus in reply, "Lord, it is good that we are here. If you wish, I will make three tents here, one for you, one for Moses, and one for Elijah." While he was still speaking, behold, a bright cloud cast a shadow over them, then from the cloud came a voice that said, "This is my beloved Son, with whom I am well pleased; listen to him."

Reflection

I have always enjoyed the experience of hiking up a mountain. The physical exercise, the opportunity to connect with nature, and the sense of accomplishment of arriving at the mountaintop are all attractive to me. There are also spiritual components of a climb, such as time for quiet and prayer, feeling closer to heaven, and looking at the grandeur of creation. Peter, James, and John must have spent a fair amount of time with Jesus as they climbed. Did they have any idea that something so significant was going to happen once they arrived at the summit? Today's reading invites us to be more aware and intentional about our journey with Jesus. When we co[...] our own spiritual lives, are we willing to put in th[...] hike the miles in prayer so that we may be pr[...] that he wishes to reveal to us?

✚ *In the name of the Father, and of t[...]*

March 8, 2026
THIRD SUNDAY OF LENT

✚ *In the name of the Father, and of the Son, and of the Holy Spirit.*

Gospel

John 4:5–10

Jesus came to a town of Samaria called Sychar, near the plot of land that Jacob had given to his son Joseph. Jacob's well was there. Jesus, tired from his journey, sat down there at the well. It was about noon.

A woman of Samaria came to draw water. Jesus said to her, "Give me a drink." His disciples had gone into the town to buy food. The Samaritan woman said to him, "How can you, a Jew, ask me, a Samaritan woman, for a drink?"—For Jews use nothing in common with Samaritans.—Jesus answered and said to her, "If you knew the gift of God and who is saying to you, 'Give me a drink,' you would have asked him and he would have given you living water."

Reflection

Thirst is a universal human experience. While we can live for many days without food, we can only live a short time without water. In today's Gospel, we find a Samaritan woman seeking to quench her thirst. Jesus builds on this foundational bodily need to introduce her to a spiritual one. Jesus describes her need for living water, a water of rebirth and salvation. Through the grace of baptism, we have access to the living water of Jesus. Each time we enter a church and sign ourselves, we are reminded of this gift and of our ongoing need for God's replenishing presence in our lives. And as we encounter the thirst for truth from our students, we are blessed to offer them true refreshment for their souls.

✚ *In the name of the Father, and of the Son, and of the Holy Spirit.*

March 15, 2026
FOURTH SUNDAY OF LENT

✚ *In the name of the Father, and of the Son, and of the Holy Spirit.*

Gospel

John 9:1–3, 6–7

As Jesus passed by he saw a man blind from birth. His disciples asked him, "Rabbi, who sinned, this man or his parents, that he was born blind?" Jesus answered, "Neither he nor his parents sinned; it is so that the works of God might be made visible through him." When he had said this, he spat on the ground and made clay with the saliva, and smeared the clay on his eyes, and said to him, "Go wash in the Pool of Siloam"—which means Sent. So he went and washed, and came back able to see.

Reflection

There are many dynamics happening in this story, but its origins are in parents who gave birth to a son with a disability, and they and their religious society are trying to make sense of why this would happen. The prevailing sentiment is that some sort of sinfulness caused this, but Jesus does not let anyone settle for such an assumption. Instead, he challenges this societal notion and shows his love for the man by not only healing his physical blindness but also revealing his divine identity to the man. As teachers of the faith, we are called to partner with Jesus in washing away the blindness of ignorance that is part of the human condition. By helping our students see Jesus clearly, we give them the chance to follow him like the man healed in today's reading.

✚ *In the name of the Father, and of the Son, and of the Holy Spirit.*

March 22, 2026
FIFTH SUNDAY OF LENT

✚ *In the name of the Father, and of the Son, and of the Holy Spirit.*

Gospel

John 11:17, 32–36

When Jesus arrived, he found that Lazarus had already been in the tomb for four days.

When Mary came to where Jesus was and saw him, she fell at his feet and said to him, "Lord, if you had been here, my brother would not have died." When Jesus saw her weeping and the Jews who had come with her weeping, he became perturbed and deeply troubled, and said, "Where have you laid him?" They said to him, "Sir, come and see." And Jesus wept. So the Jews said, "See how he loved him."

Reflection

Before Jesus raises Lazarus from death, he enters into our human suffering, feeling the sharp pang that accompanies the death of someone dear to us. Imagine the scene with Jesus, the Son of God, reduced to tears as the reality of his friend's death washes over him. When we cry to the Lord in our grief do we find it within ourselves to trust in him who knows the depth of our pain? And if one of our students faces an unexpected tragedy, can we (as Christ consoled his friends Martha and Mary) offer them consolation and love? Though we may never understand God's purpose in the face of great loss, we cling to the hope of the resurrection to follow.

✚ *In the name of the Father, and of the Son, and of the Holy Spirit.*

March 29, 2026
PALM SUNDAY OF THE PASSION OF THE LORD

✚ *In the name of the Father, and of the Son, and of the Holy Spirit.*

Gospel
Matthew 21:1–9

When Jesus and the disciples drew near Jerusalem and came to Bethphage on the Mount of Olives, Jesus sent two disciples, saying to them, "Go into the village opposite you, and immediately you will find an ass tethered, and a colt with her. Untie them and bring them here to me. And if anyone should say anything to you, reply, 'The master has need of them.' Then he will send them at once." This happened so that what had been spoken through the prophet might be fulfilled:/*Say to daughter Zion,/ "Behold, your king comes to you,/meek and riding on an ass,/and on a colt, the foal of a beast of burden."*/ The disciples went and did as Jesus had ordered them. They brought the ass and the colt and laid their cloaks over them, and he sat upon them. The very large crowd spread their cloaks on the road, while others cut branches from the trees and strewed them on the road. The crowds preceding him and those following kept crying out and saying: / "Hosanna to the Son of David; / blessed is he who comes in the name of the Lord; / hosanna in the highest."

Reflection
In entering Jerusalem, Jesus knows what lies before him. He is not a passive victim to the events of Holy Week but comes to the holy city and embraces his cross willingly out of love. Do we approach our ministry—whether it offers us accolades and praise from the people of God or a share in Christ's cross—with a willingness to serve, motivated by love for our students?

✚ *In the name of the Father, and of the Son, and of the Holy Spirit.*

April 5, 2026
EASTER SUNDAY OF THE RESURRECTION OF THE LORD

✚ *In the name of the Father, and of the Son, and of the Holy Spirit.*

Gospel

Matthew 28:1–2, 5–10

After the sabbath, as the first day of the week was dawning, Mary Magdalene and the other Mary came to see the tomb. And behold, there was a great earthquake; for an angel of the Lord descended from heaven, approached, rolled back the stone, and sat upon it. Then the angel said to the women in reply, "Do not be afraid! I know that you are seeking Jesus the crucified. He is not here, for he has been raised just as he said. Come and see the place where he lay. Then go quickly and tell his disciples, 'He has been raised from the dead, and he is going before you to Galilee; there you will see him.' Behold, I have told you." Then they went away quickly from the tomb, fearful yet overjoyed, and ran to announce this to his disciples. And behold, Jesus met them on their way and greeted them. They approached, embraced his feet, and did him homage. Then Jesus said to them, "Do not be afraid. Go tell my brothers to go to Galilee, and there they will see me."

Reflection

It is difficult to fathom how much of an emotional roller coaster it must have been for Jesus' followers in the days leading up to the resurrection. First, their leader and friend is arrested, tried, and crucified, with most of their group scattering in fear. Then, in the pervasive fog of their grief, they encounter the risen Lord. To say this was a shock would be an understatement! As catechists, do we allow the joy of Christ's resurrection—the most momentous and important event in the story of our salvation—to surprise and astound us today?

✚ *In the name of the Father, and of the Son, and of the Holy Spirit.*

April 12, 2026
SECOND SUNDAY OF EASTER / SUNDAY OF DIVINE MERCY

✚ *In the name of the Father, and of the Son, and of the Holy Spirit.*

Gospel

John 20:19–20, 24–28

On the evening of that first day of the week, when the doors were locked, where the disciples were, . . . Jesus came and stood in their midst and said to them, "Peace be with you." When he had said this, he showed them his hands and his side. The disciples rejoiced when they saw the Lord.

Thomas, called Didymus, one of the Twelve, was not with them when Jesus came. So the other disciples said to him, "We have seen the Lord." But he said to them, "Unless I see the mark of the nails in his hands and put my finger into the nailmarks and put my hand into his side, I will not believe."

Now a week later . . . Jesus came . . . and said, "Peace be with you." Then he said to Thomas, "Put your finger here and see my hands, and bring your hand and put it into my side, and do not be unbelieving, but believe." Thomas answered and said to him, "My Lord and my God!"

Reflection

It is a tough break for "doubting" Thomas that one of his weaker moments is recorded for all time in John's Gospel. Notice, though, that the story doesn't end there. Thomas later makes a heartfelt profession of faith that inspires catechists and students alike. Today's Gospel reminds us that we are ultimately not defined by our weakest moments. Though doubt is often part of the journey of faith, God is always willing to meet us where we are and draw us closer to himself.

✚ *In the name of the Father, and of the Son, and of the Holy Spirit.*

April 19, 2026
THIRD SUNDAY OF EASTER

✚ *In the name of the Father, and of the Son, and of the Holy Spirit.*

Gospel

Luke 24:13, 30–35

That very day, the first day of the week, two of Jesus' disciples were going to a village seven miles from Jerusalem called Emmaus. . . . And it happened that, while he was with them at table, he took bread, said the blessing, broke it, and gave it to them. With that their eyes were opened and they recognized him, but he vanished from their sight. Then they said to each other, "Were not our hearts burning with us while he spoke to us on the way and opened the Scriptures to us?" So they set out at once and returned to Jerusalem where they found gathered together the eleven and those with them who were saying, "The Lord has truly been raised and has appeared to Simon!" Then the two recounted what had taken place on the way and how he was made known to them in the breaking of bread.

Reflection

There are times when we are so ecstatic to share news that we can hardly do anything else. Being accepted into a dream school, sharing an accepted wedding proposal, and being hired for a sought-after job are only a few of the times when our enthusiasm overflows in the retelling. The disciples who encountered Jesus on the road to Emmaus had a moment like this. They had been so blinded by their sadness that they did not recognize Jesus until the Eucharistic moment of the story, and then he was gone. Overcome with amazement and joy, they race back to Jerusalem to share the news. What about our faith moves us enough that we want to share it with others with fervor and passion?

✚ *In the name of the Father, and of the Son, and of the Holy Spirit.*

April 26, 2026
FOURTH SUNDAY OF EASTER

✚ *In the name of the Father, and of the Son, and of the Holy Spirit.*

Gospel

John 10:1–5, 7–10

Jesus said, "Amen, amen, I say to you, whoever does not enter a sheepfold through the gate but climbs over elsewhere is a thief and a robber. But whoever enters through the gate is the shepherd of the sheep. The gatekeeper opens it for him, and the sheep hear his voice, as the shepherd calls his own sheep by name and leads them out. When he has driven out all his own, he walks ahead of them, and the sheep follow him, because they recognize his voice. But they will not follow a stranger; they will run away from him, because they do not recognize the voice of strangers."

. . . "Amen, amen, I say to you, I am the gate for the sheep. All who came before me are thieves and robbers, but the sheep did not listen to them. I am the gate. Whoever enters through me will be saved, and will come in and go out and find pasture. A thief comes only to steal and slaughter and destroy; I came so that they might have life and have it more abundantly."

Reflection

In today's Gospel, Jesus, the Good Shepherd, shares what it means to be a good leader. It is not about wielding power and influence, forcing followers into submission. Instead, servant leaders are willing to make great sacrifices for those in their care. In speaking of the shepherd who is willing to lay down his life for his sheep, Jesus foreshadows what he will do on the cross for us. Our task, as the sheep of the Lord, is to be willing to listen to and follow his voice. As catechists, we also accept the task of leading others to the verdant pastures of his love.

✚ *In the name of the Father, and of the Son, and of the Holy Spirit.*

May 3, 2026
FIFTH SUNDAY OF EASTER

✚ *In the name of the Father, and of the Son, and of the Holy Spirit.*

Gospel

John 14:1–9

Jesus said to his disciples: "Do not let your hearts be troubled. You have faith in God; have faith also in me. In my Father's house there are many dwelling places. If there were not, would I have told you that I am going to prepare a place for you? And if I go and prepare a place for you, I will come back again and take you to myself, so that where I am you also may be. Where I am going you know the way." Thomas said to him, "Master, we do not know where you are going; how can we know the way?" Jesus said to him, "I am the way and the truth and the life. No one comes to the Father except through me. If you know me, then you will also know my Father. From now on you do know him and have seen him." Philip said to him, "Master, show us the Father, and that will be enough for us." Jesus said to him, "Have I been with you for so long a time and you still do not know me, Philip? Whoever has seen me has seen the Father."

Reflection

What are the reasons that our hearts might be troubled? There might be financial pressures, relationship problems, societal tragedies, or even the fear of death. We may also be struggling to reach a student in our class or know how to help them with a problem they are facing. Jesus reassures his followers and us that by knowing him, we know God the Father, and that we are all in his loving care. It is truly a comfort to consider that, at the end of the strife of our lives, a place is prepared for us in heaven. We live, then, as a people of hope.

✚ *In the name of the Father, and of the Son, and of the Holy Spirit.*

May 10, 2026
SIXTH SUNDAY OF EASTER

✚ *In the name of the Father, and of the Son, and of the Holy Spirit.*

Gospel

John 14:15–20

Jesus said to his disciples: "If you love me, you will keep my commandments. And I will ask the Father, and he will give you another Advocate to be with you always, the Spirit of truth, whom the world cannot accept, because it neither sees nor knows him. But you know him, because he remains with you, and will be in you. I will not leave you orphans; I will come to you. In a little while the world will no longer see me, but you will see me, because I live and you will live. On that day you will realize that I am in my Father and you are in me and I in you."

Reflection

One of the skills that boy scouts learn is called orienteering, where a scout navigates an area using a map, compass, and the features of the natural world. The hope is that a scout will become proficient enough to use this skill without the help of an adult. I think orienteering is a good image to think about when considering Jesus' gift of the Spirit in today's reading. Jesus has been with his disciples for a few years, but he knows it will not last forever. After his resurrection, Jesus will only be with them for a short while before returning to the Father. But just as a scout is left with tools to navigate unknown terrain, Jesus promises to send the Holy Spirit to help his followers on their journey back to God. As catechists, our task is to trust the Holy Spirit to guide us, even as we navigate uncertainty in our lives, and to teach our students to do likewise.

✚ *In the name of the Father, and of the Son, and of the Holy Spirit.*

May 14/17, 2026
SOLEMNITY OF THE ASCENSION OF THE LORD

✚ *In the name of the Father, and of the Son, and of the Holy Spirit.*

Gospel

Matthew 28:16–20

The eleven disciples went to Galilee, to the mountain to which Jesus had ordered them. When they saw him, they worshiped, but they doubted. Then Jesus approached and said to them, "All power in heaven and on earth has been given to me. Go, therefore, and make disciples of all nations, baptizing them in the name of the Father, and of the Son, and of the Holy Spirit, teaching them to observe all that I have commanded you. And behold, I am with you always, until the end of the age."

Reflection

Goodbyes can be difficult moments. Whether it is sending a child to school on the first day of kindergarten, leaving home for college, or a final hospital visit to an ailing loved one, we know well the difficulty of a goodbye. Jesus' disciples felt this too at his ascension. There must have been some sadness in the group as they said a final farewell to Jesus. Knowing the human heart well, Jesus reassured them with a promise to remain close to them. And although we can no longer see Jesus in his human form, we still believe that his presence is with us, especially in the Eucharist. This is a gift that is in every tabernacle around the world, and it helps us as the Church to carry out Christ's command to share the Gospel to every nation. We can be confident that, even when the inevitable partings of life take place, we will always be united in Christ beyond time and space.

✚ *In the name of the Father, and of the Son, and of the Holy Spirit.*

May 17, 2026
SEVENTH SUNDAY OF EASTER

✚ *In the name of the Father, and of the Son, and of the Holy Spirit.*

Gospel

John 17:1–9, 10a

Jesus raised his eyes to heaven and said, "Father, the hour has come. Give glory to your son, so that your son may glorify you, just as you gave him authority over all people, so that he may give eternal life to all you gave him. Now this is eternal life, that they should know you, the only true God, and the one whom you sent, Jesus Christ. I glorified you on earth by accomplishing the work that you gave me to do. Now glorify me, Father, with you, with the glory that I had with you before the world began.

"I revealed your name to those whom you gave me out of the world. They belonged to you, and you gave them to me, and they have kept your word. Now they know that everything you gave me is from you, because the words you gave to me I have given to them, and they accepted them and truly understood that I came from you, and they have believed that you sent me. I pray for . . . the ones you have given me, because they are yours, and everything of mine is yours and everything of yours is mine."

Reflection

The relationship between a parent and child is built on a foundation of love. Even before a baby is born, a parent's natural inclination is to love and nurture. Due to our human sinfulness, that love is not always perfect, but we have a model of perfection in the transcendent relationship between the Father and the Son. Notice in today's Gospel how intimately Jesus speaks with his Father. As catechists, our task is to introduce and share that unconditional love with our students and their families.

✚ *In the name of the Father, and of the Son, and of the Holy Spirit.*

May 24, 2026
SOLEMNITY OF PENTECOST

✚ *In the name of the Father, and of the Son, and of the Holy Spirit.*

Gospel

John 20:19–23

On the evening of that first day of the week, when the doors were locked, where the disciples were, for fear of the Jews, Jesus came and stood in their midst and said to them, "Peace be with you." When he had said this, he showed them his hands and his side. The disciples rejoiced when they saw the Lord. Jesus said to them again, "Peace be with you. As the Father has sent me, so I send you." And when he had said this, he breathed on them and said to them, "Receive the Holy Spirit. Whose sins you forgive are forgiven them, and whose sins you retain are retained."

Reflection

Pentecost is an important celebration marking the beginning of the rapid expansion of the faith throughout the world. Had the followers of Jesus remained fearful and locked in rooms, the Church would have gone out with a pious, gradual whimper. Instead, the opposite happened due to Jesus' gift of the Holy Spirit. Soon the apostles would travel across the world to preach the Gospel to all who would listen. We are the inheritors of that legacy, and it is now our turn to provide that gift to the next generation. What things about our faith do we still keep locked away and hidden due to our fear? How can we ask the Holy Spirit to enter into our lives so that we can find the courage we may lack?

✚ *In the name of the Father, and of the Son, and of the Holy Spirit.*

May 31, 2026
SOLEMNITY OF THE MOST HOLY TRINITY

✚ *In the name of the Father, and of the Son, and of the Holy Spirit.*

Gospel
John 3:16–18

God so loved the world that he gave his only Son, so that everyone who believes in him might not perish but might have eternal life. For God did not send his Son into the world to condemn the world, but that the world might be saved through him. Whoever believes in him will not be condemned, but whoever does not believe has already been condemned, because he has not believed in the name of the only Son of God.

Reflection

Many popular songs are filled with notions of human love, the singer conveying the lengths one would go to show affection. Of course, this sort of love may be more infatuation and can quickly fade, or it is conditional and only lasts as long as the relationship continues as expected. What are the limits of our willingness to love? Would instances of betrayal, infidelity, anger, and ridicule diminish our ability to love? The answer for most human beings would be yes. But God's love is radically different. Despite our unfaithfulness, God's response is to love us all the more, to send his Son to be our teacher and redeemer. How great must God's love be for each one of us to send us such a gift! What a beautiful task we have—to help others to understand the depth of this divine love!

✚ *In the name of the Father, and of the Son, and of the Holy Spirit.*

June 7, 2026
SOLEMNITY OF THE MOST HOLY BODY AND BLOOD OF CHRIST

✚ *In the name of the Father, and of the Son, and of the Holy Spirit.*

Gospel

John 6:51–58

[Jesus said to the crowds:] "I am the living bread that came down from heaven; whoever eats this bread will live forever; and the bread that I will give is my flesh for the life of the world."

The Jews quarreled among themselves, saying, "How can this man give us his flesh to eat?" Jesus said to them, "Amen, amen, I say to you, unless you eat the flesh of the Son of Man and drink his blood, you do not have life within you. Whoever eats my flesh and drinks my blood has eternal life, and I will raise him on the last day. For my flesh is true food, and my blood is true drink. Whoever eats my flesh and drinks my blood remains in me and I in him. Just as the living Father sent me and I have life because of the Father, so also the one who feeds on me will have life because of me. This is the bread that came down from heaven. Unlike your ancestors who ate and still died, whoever eats this bread will live forever."

Reflection

So long ago, Jesus gave us the gift of his Body and Blood—first at the Last Supper and then on the cross. In the Eucharist, we are drawn into an intimate union with our Savior and we share in the grace of those sacred events. Today's readings remind us to give thanks for this precious gift and invite us to recommit ourselves to sharing its power and sustaining love with others.

✚ *In the name of the Father, and of the Son, and of the Holy Spirit.*

June 14, 2026
ELEVENTH SUNDAY IN ORDINARY TIME

✚ *In the name of the Father, and of the Son, and of the Holy Spirit.*

Gospel

Matthew 10:5–8

Jesus sent out the twelve after instructing them thus, "Do not go into pagan territory or enter a Samaritan town. Go rather to the lost sheep of the house of Israel. As you go, make this proclamation: 'The kingdom of heaven is at hand.' Cure the sick, raise the dead, cleanse lepers, drive out demons. Without cost you have received; without cost you are to give."

Reflection

Anyone who has flown in an airplane has heard the instructions "Please put on your own oxygen mask before assisting others." The first time I heard this, I was somewhat taken aback, thinking that it sounded a bit selfish. In time, I realized that I would not be of any help to others if I was unconscious due to lack of oxygen. In today's Gospel, Jesus tells the disciples to go only to the lost sheep of Israel—essentially, to tend to their own people first. This would not preclude them from going to foreign lands to share the Gospel at a later time, but for now, this is what Jesus instructed. Often in ministry, we say, "You cannot give what you do not have." Take some time this day to attend to your own spiritual needs. If we are spiritually depleted, how can we hope to evangelize others?

✚ *In the name of the Father, and of the Son, and of the Holy Spirit.*

June 21, 2026
TWELFTH SUNDAY IN ORDINARY TIME

✚ *In the name of the Father, and of the Son, and of the Holy Spirit.*

Gospel *Matthew 10:26–33*

Jesus said to the Twelve: "Fear no one. Nothing is concealed that will not be revealed, nor secret that will not be known. What I say to you in the darkness, speak in the light; what you hear whispered, proclaim on the housetops. And do not be afraid of those who kill the body but cannot kill the soul; rather, be afraid of the one who can destroy both soul and body in Gehenna. Are not two sparrows sold for a small coin? Yet not one of them falls to the ground without your Father's knowledge. Even all the hairs of your head are counted. So do not be afraid; you are worth more than many sparrows. Everyone who acknowledges me before others I will acknowledge before my heavenly Father. But whoever denies me before others, I will deny before my heavenly Father."

Reflection

There are periods in life that can bring about great anxiety, occasions that leave us staring at the ceiling at night, unable to sleep. In the midst of such turmoil, one option we have is to turn to God in prayer. This practice often brings peace and calm, even if many aspects of the situation remain out of our control. In today's Gospel, Jesus encourages us to see things from God's eternal perspective. From that vantage point, no suffering that we will endure in this life can compare with the happiness offered to us in the next. The next time we are filled with life's worries, how can we place our trust in God and rest in the certain hope that we are beloved beyond measure?

✚ *In the name of the Father, and of the Son, and of the Holy Spirit.*

June 28, 2026
THIRTEENTH SUNDAY IN ORDINARY TIME

✚ *In the name of the Father, and of the Son, and of the Holy Spirit.*

Gospel

Matthew 10:37–42

Jesus said to his apostles: "Whoever loves father or mother more than me is not worthy of me, and whoever loves son or daughter more than me is not worthy of me; and whoever does not take up his cross and follow after me is not worthy of me. Whoever finds his life will lose it, and whoever loses his life for my sake will find it.

"Whoever receives you receives me, and whoever receives me receives the one who sent me. Whoever receives a prophet because he is a prophet will receive a prophet's reward, and whoever receives a righteous man because he is righteous will receive a righteous man's reward. And whoever gives only a cup of cold water to one of these little ones to drink because he is a disciple—amen, I say to you, he will surely not lose his reward."

Reflection

Each of us is called to build up the kingdom of God. To do this, some will be called to forms of radical discipleship that look foolish to the world. Pursuing one's God-given vocation can require us to live far away from our loved ones or to make decisions that others may not always understand. Despite the sacrifices we make in pursuing God's will, we know that following the desires God has placed in our hearts will lead to tremendous good for others and will bring us lasting joy.

✚ *In the name of the Father, and of the Son, and of the Holy Spirit.*

JULY 5, 2026
FOURTEENTH SUNDAY IN ORDINARY TIME

✚ *In the name of the Father, and of the Son, and of the Holy Spirit.*

GOSPEL

Matthew 11:25–30

At that time Jesus exclaimed: "I give praise to you, Father, Lord of heaven and earth, for although you have hidden these things from the wise and the learned you have revealed them to little ones. Yes, Father, such has been your gracious will. All things have been handed over to me by my Father. No one knows the Son except the Father, and no one knows the Father except the Son and anyone to whom the Son wishes to reveal him.

"Come to me, all you who labor and are burdened, and I will give you rest. Take my yoke upon you and learn from me, for I am meek and humble of heart; and you will find rest for yourselves. For my yoke is easy, and my burden light."

REFLECTION

Sometimes, the demands of the Christian life can seem overwhelming, and yet in today's Gospel, Jesus describes his yoke as easy and his burden light. At first glance, this seems counterintuitive to our experiences. What is easy to forget, though, is how much our life in Christ provides for us. Imagine for a moment what it would be like to go through life without a community of faith to support us, without the grace of the sacraments to sustain us, and without the hope and promise of eternal life. This awareness is a large part of the reason we share faith with others, including our students. No one should go through life without the consolation of knowing that we are loved and that we do not carry the burdens we face alone.

✚ *In the name of the Father, and of the Son, and of the Holy Spirit.*

July 12, 2026
FIFTEENTH SUNDAY IN ORDINARY TIME

✚ *In the name of the Father, and of the Son, and of the Holy Spirit.*

Gospel
Matthew 13:10–13

The disciples approached [Jesus] and said, "Why do you speak to them in parables?" He said to them in reply, "Because knowledge of the mysteries of the kingdom of heaven has been granted to you, but to them it has not been granted. To anyone who has, more will be given and he will grow rich; from anyone who has not, even what he has will be taken away. This is why I speak to them in parables, because 'they look but do not see and hear but do not listen or understand.'"

Reflection
We are offered so many options of entertainment today that it can be rare to simply sit and listen to a well-told story. In the days of Jesus, storytelling would have been one of the main sources of entertainment. Yet Jesus used stories and parables for an even higher purpose; he used them to help people understand the things of God. We know that stories are easy to remember and share with others, but we cheat ourselves and those we teach if we fail to uncover their deeper meaning. Ever the master teacher, Jesus encourages his disciples to listen to and discover the true meaning of his parables. Let's ask him for the grace to do the same as we listen to and share these stories with our students.

✚ *In the name of the Father, and of the Son, and of the Holy Spirit.*

July 19, 2026
SIXTEENTH SUNDAY IN ORDINARY TIME

✚ *In the name of the Father, and of the Son, and of the Holy Spirit.*

Gospel

Matthew 13:31–33

Jesus proposed another parable to them. “The kingdom of heaven is like a mustard seed that a person took and sowed in a field. It is the smallest of all the seeds, yet when full-grown it is the largest of plants. It becomes a large bush, and the ‘birds of the sky come and dwell in its branches.’”

He spoke to them another parable. “The kingdom of heaven is like yeast that a woman took and mixed with three measures of wheat flour until the whole batch was leavened.”

Reflection

From the time I was young, bread making machines have been quite popular. The promise of these machines is that they make homemade bread much more easily than traditional methods. Perhaps what was lost in the convenience, however, was witnessing the interplay of the ingredients to make the perfect loaf. Yeast takes time to have its full effect, and there is kneading and waiting that has to happen when bread is made by hand. In today’s Gospel, Jesus uses the example of small things—like mustard seeds and yeast—that have a large effect on their surroundings. Are there little hints of God’s grace, present in the people and ordinary circumstances of our lives, that we are overlooking? What steps could we take to notice and contribute to small acts of faith and kindness that could significantly better the world around us?

✚ *In the name of the Father, and of the Son, and of the Holy Spirit.*

July 26, 2026
SEVENTEENTH SUNDAY IN ORDINARY TIME

✚ *In the name of the Father, and of the Son, and of the Holy Spirit.*

Gospel

Matthew 13:44–49a, 51–52

Jesus said to his disciples: "The kingdom of heaven is like a treasure buried in a field, which a person finds and hides again, and out of joy goes and sells all that he has and buys that field. Again, the kingdom of heaven is like a merchant searching for fine pearls. When he finds a pearl of great price, he goes and sells all that he has and buys it. Again, the kingdom of heaven is like a net thrown into the sea, which collects fish of every kind. When it is full they haul it ashore and sit down to put what is good into buckets. What is bad they throw away. Thus it will be at the end of the age.

"Do you understand all these things?" They answered, "Yes." And he replied, "Then every scribe who has been instructed in the kingdom of heaven is like the head of a household who brings from his storeroom both the new and the old."

Reflection

Every so often, there are news articles about a person purchasing something like a piece of art or a book that turns out to be worth much more than what the buyer originally paid. There also seem to be a number of shows on television that have the premise of discovering rare finds in places like attics, storage units, and old barns. The fascination with these stories seems to be that we love the idea of finding something valuable when others have discarded it. Our faith is often like that. The world does not see the wisdom in going to great lengths to practice and live our faith, but as believers, we know that we have something with value beyond measure.

✚ *In the name of the Father, and of the Son, and of the Holy Spirit.*

AUGUST 2, 2026
EIGHTEENTH SUNDAY IN ORDINARY TIME

✚ *In the name of the Father, and of the Son, and of the Holy Spirit.*

GOSPEL

Matthew 14:13–21

When Jesus heard of the death of John the Baptist, he withdrew in a boat to a deserted place by himself. The crowds heard of this and followed him on foot from their towns. When he disembarked and saw the vast crowd, his heart was moved with pity for them, and he cured their sick. When it was evening, the disciples approached him and said, "This is a deserted place and it is already late; dismiss the crowds so that they can go to the villages and buy food for themselves." Jesus said to them, "There is no need for them to go away; give them some food yourselves." But they said to him, "Five loaves and two fish are all we have here." Then he said, "Bring them here to me," and he ordered the crowds to sit down on the grass. Taking the five loaves and the two fish, and looking up to heaven, he said the blessing, broke the loaves, and gave them to the disciples, who in turn gave them to the crowds. They all ate and were satisfied, and they picked up the fragments left over—twelve wicker baskets full. Those who ate were about five thousand men, not counting women and children.

REFLECTION

Today's Gospel begins with Jesus mourning the death of his cousin, John the Baptist. Nevertheless, the crowds do not allow him to grieve for very long, and he is soon moved with compassion for them. Jesus performs healings and miracles, culminating in the feeding of thousands of people. As catechists, we know what it means to offer ourselves even when we are not at our best, and we follow Jesus' example by offering his spiritual nourishment to others.

✚ *In the name of the Father, and of the Son, and of the Holy Spirit.*

August 9, 2026
NINETEENTH SUNDAY IN ORDINARY TIME

✚ *In the name of the Father, and of the Son, and of the Holy Spirit.*

Gospel
Matthew 14:26–33

When the disciples saw [Jesus] walking on the sea they were terrified. "It is a ghost," they said, and they cried out in fear. At once Jesus spoke to them, "Take courage, it is I; do not be afraid." Peter said to him in reply, "Lord, if it is you, command me to come to you on the water." He said, "Come." Peter got out of the boat and began to walk on the water toward Jesus. But when he saw how strong the wind was he became frightened; and, beginning to sink, he cried out, "Lord, save me!" Immediately Jesus stretched out his hand and caught Peter, and said to him, "O you of little faith, why did you doubt?" After they got into the boat, the wind died down. Those who were in the boat did him homage, saying, "Truly, you are the Son of God."

Reflection

In today's Gospel, the wind and the waves of the storm at sea distract Peter from recognizing the incredible reality that he and Jesus were walking on water! What are the aspects of our lives that take our gaze away from God and what God is doing? Do we see our students worrying about things to the point that they forget who is the source of all that is good in our lives? Let us recommit ourselves to looking into the eyes of Jesus with confidence and encouraging others to do likewise. After all, Jesus is more powerful than any storms that may rage around us!

✚ *In the name of the Father, and of the Son, and of the Holy Spirit.*

August 16, 2026
TWENTIETH SUNDAY IN ORDINARY TIME

✚ *In the name of the Father, and of the Son, and of the Holy Spirit.*

Gospel

Matthew 15:21–28

At that time, Jesus withdrew to the region of Tyre and Sidon. And behold, a Canaanite woman of that district came and called out, "Have pity on me, Lord, Son of David! My daughter is tormented by a demon." But Jesus did not say a word in answer to her. His disciples came and asked him, "Send her away, for she keeps calling out after us." He said in reply, "I was sent only to the lost sheep of the house of Israel." But the woman came and did Jesus homage, saying, "Lord, help me." He said in reply, "It is not right to take the food of the children and throw it to the dogs." She said, "Please, Lord, for even the dogs eat the scraps that fall from the table of their masters." Then Jesus said to her in reply, "O woman, great is your faith! Let it be done for you as you wish." And the woman's daughter was healed from that hour.

Reflection

Dog owners know well the look of pleading that comes from our pets in search of food. The big eyes, tilted head, and soft whimper make it clear what a dog wants. Because we love our animals, it is sometimes difficult to refuse them. In today's Gospel, the Canaanite woman compares herself to a dog seeking scraps from the table. While others might have used the word *dog* to label her as an outsider, she adopts it to make an appeal that pulls on Jesus' heartstrings. Her persistence demonstrates an unshakable faith that Jesus will give her what she asks—a request that Jesus finds impossible to ignore. How might we come to the Lord with the kind of faith this woman possessed, knowing that he loves us unconditionally?

✚ *In the name of the Father, and of the Son, and of the Holy Spirit.*

August 23, 2026
TWENTY-FIRST SUNDAY IN ORDINARY TIME

✚ *In the name of the Father, and of the Son, and of the Holy Spirit.*

Gospel
Matthew 16:15–18

[Jesus said to his disciples:] "But who do you say that I am?" Simon Peter said in reply, "You are the Christ, the Son of the living God." Jesus said to him in reply, "Blessed are you, Simon son of Jonah. For flesh and blood has not revealed this to you, but my heavenly Father. And so I say to you, you are Peter, and upon this rock I will build my church, and the gates of the netherworld shall not prevail against it."

Reflection
Growing up in western Kansas, I grew accustomed to severe storms in the summertime. Cool air coming off the Rocky Mountains would pick up moisture and—combined with heat from the sun—produce lightning, thunder, rain, and hail, as well as the occasional tornado. When the sirens would sound in town, our family would go to the basement and shelter under the stairs. During those episodes, I was thankful to have a home with a strong foundation to keep us safe.

In today's Gospel, Jesus promises that the Church will be able to withstand all things opposed to it. Despite the challenges the Church has faced in her history, we stand on the firm foundation built by Christ. Together with the many holy men and women who have come before us, we take our place in building up the Church, resting on the unshakable foundation of our faith.

✚ *In the name of the Father, and of the Son, and of the Holy Spirit.*

August 30, 2026
TWENTY-SECOND SUNDAY IN ORDINARY TIME

✚ *In the name of the Father, and of the Son, and of the Holy Spirit.*

Gospel

Matthew 16:21–24

Jesus began to show his disciples that he must go to Jerusalem and suffer greatly from the elders, the chief priests, and the scribes, and be killed and on the third day be raised. Then Peter took Jesus aside and began to rebuke him, "God forbid, Lord! No such thing shall ever happen to you." He turned and said to Peter, "Get behind me, Satan! You are an obstacle to me. You are thinking not as God does, but as human beings do."

Then Jesus said to his disciples, "Whoever wishes to come after me must deny himself, take up his cross, and follow me."

Reflection

Many have seen videos online of athletes making embarrassing mistakes on the field. I remember watching one in which a football player ran down the field about to score a touchdown, only to drop the ball on the two yard line in premature celebration.

In a sense, Peter makes an error like this in our story today. Last week, we heard about Peter's wonderful profession of faith, and how Jesus named him the leader of the Church. In today's reading, we see Peter contradicting Jesus as he predicts his suffering and death. Jesus sharply rebukes him, reminding him that God's plans do not always match human ones. Even though others look to us as leaders in faith due to our catechetical ministry, we would do well to approach this role with humility. Though given authority, we are not immune to human weakness and error. We are called to trust in and rely on God's wisdom—rather than our own.

✚ *In the name of the Father, and of the Son, and of the Holy Spirit.*

ABOUT THE AUTHOR

Daniel J. Allen is an author and speaker on various topics of the Catholic faith, including evangelization, vocational discernment, and accompaniment through suffering. Having experience in campus ministry, retreats, and catechetical efforts, he currently serves as the Associate Director of Spirituality and Service for the University of Notre Dame Alumni Association. In this role, he oversees FaithND, a digital evangelization effort for Notre Dame alumni, parents, and friends. He has been featured on several of FaithND's media campaigns, including a pilgrimage to the Holy Land video series, various seasonal projects for Advent and Lent, and as the host of the Everyday Holiness podcast. His writing and work have also been presented on foryourmarriage.org, grottonetwork.com, and EWTN. He is the coauthor of *Ghost Stories from the Samaritan House*, author of *Stations of the Cross for Marriages and Families*, and a contributing writer to the *Notre Dame Book of Prayer: Updated Edition*. He lives in Granger, Indiana, with his wife, Stephanie, and their children.